Framework FOCUS

YEAR **7**

Grammar

Louis Fidge
Ray Barker

How to use this book

Letts Framework Focus: Grammar books have been designed to provide a versatile resource, capable of being used for a variety of teaching and learning situations and by a wide range of teachers – specialists and non-specialists alike. They:

- contain 30 units of work, sufficient for one school year
- are straightforward and easy to use
- provide discrete double-page spread format for quick reference
- have a clear teaching focus
- contain differentiated activities for each objective.

Letts Framework Focus: Grammar books can be used in a variety of ways:

- They easily provide work for the whole class, groups or individuals.
- Use them to introduce a key literacy topic – as a lesson 'starter'.
- The structure of the pages allows for teaching a particular literacy issue to the whole class.
- Units allow teachers to focus on a particular issue if this seems a problem for an individual or group.
- Planned progression allows teachers to consolidate, develop and extend literacy work over the year.
- Each unit provides work for follow-up homework assignments.

As a lesson starter

The Grammar Focus provides a clear explanation of each objective with examples for discussion or illustration. Appropriate activities may be chosen from the range of differentiated tasks for discussion, or to work through with the class.

Group and individual work

These books are ideal for group and individual work. Teaching on the same subject can be realistically matched appropriately to individual pupils' abilities, allowing pupils to work independently.

Homework

The design of the material in the books provides an ideal solution to meaningful homework assignments – differentiated appropriately for each pupil.

Contents Year 7 Grammar

Unit 1: Nouns

Grammar Focus

- A **noun** is a **naming** word.
- **Common nouns** are the names of **people, places or things**:

  a girl, the park, a dragon.

- A **proper noun** is the name of a **particular** person, place or thing. Proper nouns begin with **capital** letters:

  France, Jenny.

- A **collective noun** is a name of a **group** of things or people:

  a swarm of bees, an army, a flock.

- An **abstract noun** is the name of a **feeling** or an **idea**:

  love, jealousy, anger.

- It is usually possible to put an '**article**' such as 'a', 'an' or 'the' before common, collective or abstract nouns.

Starter >

❶ Look at the box of nouns below.

park	Wednesday
James	bus
The Beatles	wasp
doctor	Mars
California	pyramid

Copy and complete the chart by sorting the nouns from the box.

Common nouns	Proper nouns

Practice >>

2 Do you know which proper nouns are being described in (a) to (f) below?

(**a**) The name of the biggest desert in Africa.
(**b**) A famous ruler of Ancient Egypt whose tomb contained a golden bed.
(**c**) People who live in Norway. (**d**) The river that flows through London.
(**e**) A large metal tower in Paris. (**f**) The capital of Scotland.

The answers are in the box below. You will have to unscramble them first and write them correctly with an initial capital letter!

uaaukttnhmn	aashra	ifeelf
naernwgois	hmetas	hrdnbeiug

REMEMBER

Don't forget to begin proper nouns with capital letters.

3 Find the collective nouns for 'a lot of' in these examples.
Use the clues and your dictionary to help.

(**a**) a lot of cattle (h _ _ _)   (**d**) a lot of ships (f _ _ _ _)
(**b**) a lot of fish (s _ _ _ _)   (**e**) a lot of soldiers (a _ _ _)
(**c**) a lot of people about to riot (m _ _)   (**f**) a lot of wolves (p _ _ _)

Extension >>>

4 Copy and complete the chart.
Change the adjectives to abstract nouns.
Use your dictionary to help.

Adjectives	Abstract nouns	Adjectives	Abstract nouns
beautiful	beauty	good	
brave		young	
hard		strong	
faithful		friendly	
courageous		lonely	
intelligent			

Feedback ↩

Nouns are labels for things that exist in the world. To see whether a word is a noun or not, try putting an 'article' ('a', 'an' or 'the') in front of it.

Objective ·····>

- To revise work on verbs and investigate verb tenses.

Grammar Focus

- Every sentence must have a **verb**. A sentence does **not make sense** without one. A verb may be an '**action**' word or a '**being**' word. In the example below, the first verb is an 'action' verb, and the second verb is a 'being' verb.

  The dog <u>chased</u> the postman. The postman <u>was</u> terrified.

- The **tense** of a verb tells you **when** the action took place in time.

  I <u>am driving</u> my car in the country.

  This is happening **now**, so the verb is in the **present** tense.

  Yesterday I <u>drove</u> my car in the country.

  This happened in the **past**, so the verb is in the **past** tense.

Starter >

❶ Copy the poem. Underline the verbs.

> Bells tinkle, bells clang
> Doors creak, doors bang,
> Bells peal, bells clang.
> Doors open, doors slam,
> Steps shuffle, steps trip.
> Paper rustles, paper rips.
> Hands rub, hands shake,
> Voices whisper, voices quake.
> Eyes stare, eyes peep,
> Children sing, children sleep.

❷ Think of five verbs that describe what each of these people do. Write them in a sentence. The first one is done for you.

- (a) A footballer jumps, runs, kicks, dives and heads a ball.
- (b) a secretary
- (c) a fire-fighter
- (d) a singer in a band
- (e) an author
- (f) a teacher

Practice ≫

3 Copy and complete the chart to show the past tense of some verbs. Be careful with the spelling. A dictionary may help.

Today I …	Yesterday I …	Today I …	Yesterday I …
play – am playing	played	speak	
jump		laugh	
shout		walk	
write		sit	
begin		grab	

4 Rewrite these sentences. Identify the verbs and change each into the past tense.

a) I sing in the bath.
b) I sit at my desk.
c) I pop all the balloons.
d) I carry a heavy bag.
e) I begin the book.
f) I copy all the correct spellings.
g) I leave the house at 8 o'clock.
h) I grab my bag from the kitchen.
i) I supply all my friends with football programmes.
j) I think they are a great team.

Extension ≫≫

5 The past tense of the verb in each sentence below is incorrect.
Rewrite each sentence correctly.

a) I buyed a lot of presents on holiday.
b) The goalkeeper catched the ball.
c) My mum leaved her bag on the train.
d) The thief stealed the video from our house.
e) The children all drinked their milk quickly.
f) The water on the lake freezed over last night.
g) Apparently, the ghost shaked all its chains to scare the visitors.
h) 'Who ringed my bell?' Mrs Reynolds sayed.
i) My sister weeped quietly at the film.

REMEMBER

To see whether a word is a verb or not, put 'to' in front of it.

Feedback ↻

Be careful when you choose verbs for your writing. Use a thesaurus if necessary. Often verbs need an 'auxiliary' or 'helper' verb to show tense or mood. For example: *will be, do, is, should, can.*

Unit 3: Tenses

Objective ·····>

- To revise and extend work on verbs, focusing on tenses.

Grammar Focus

- The **tense** of a verb tells us whether something is happening in the **past**, the **present** or the **future**.

  Present: *Now I <u>see</u> my mum.*

  Past: *Yesterday I <u>saw</u> my mum.*

  Future: *Tomorrow I <u>will see</u> my mum.*

- To enable you to communicate in the correct 'time' with your reader you need to know about tenses.

- Different types of text tend to use different tenses. For example, when you tell a story you are generally talking about the past. When you give information you are talking directly to your reader in the present. If you were giving a weather forecast you would use the future tense to express your views.

Starter >

❶ Look at the verbs in the box below.

I ran	we sail	I am
she sees	we looked	he had
he stood	I sing	you make
they write	she came	she reads
they pushed	you sell	we watched

Now use the verbs to complete this chart.

Present tense (today ...)	Past tense (yesterday ...)
I run	I ran

Practice >>

2 Copy and complete the verb chart.

To jump		To be	
Present tense	Past tense	Present tense	Past tense
I jump	I jumped	I am	I was
You	You	You	You
He/she jumps	He/she	He/she is	He/she
We	We	We	We
They	They	They	They

3 Write sentences using the 'you', 'she' and 'they' form of the verb 'to be', in the present and the past tense.

Extension >>>

4 Write out these sentences using the verb in the past tense.

REMEMBER

Re-read things you write and check that you have used verb tenses correctly.

(a) After the match the manager (to say) that the other team were lucky.

(b) It took him two years, but Glen finally (to write) his novel.

(c) Police searched all week but they never (to find) the missing necklace.

(d) You could tell he loved the baby by the way he (to hold) it.

(e) 'I have (to teach) you for a term and am proud of your exam results,' said our teacher.

5 Make up some sentences of your own, using these verbs in the past tense.

(a) to swim   (c) to begin   (e) to go
(b) to have   (d) to see

Feedback

Most of the time it is best to stick to one tense in your writing. Decide when it is appropriate to change tenses. For example, if you were writing an argument you might use more than one tense: *I am convinced of this and I am sure you will be.*

Objectives ····>

- To identify adverbs and understand their functions in sentences.
- To extend the control of more complex sentences.

Grammar Focus

- An **adverb** tells us **more about a verb**. It **describes** or **modifies** the verb in some way.
- **Most** (but not all) adverbs end with the suffix '**ly**'.

The captain proudly received the cup.

- There are four categories of adverb:

–**Time adverbs** tell us when something happens.

He runs later.

–**Place adverbs** tell us where something happens.

He runs far.

–**Manner adverbs** tell us how something happens.

He runs fast.

–**Degree adverbs** add more information about another adverb.

He runs very quickly.

Starter >

❶ Copy these sentences.
Underline the adverb in each sentence.
Circle the verb that each modifies.

ⓐ The lion roared noisily.
ⓑ The man sneezed loudly at the table.
ⓒ I answered all the questions correctly.
ⓓ The girl smiled sweetly at her grandmother.
ⓔ Shireen gazed longingly at the toys in the shop window.
ⓕ We all completed the exercises easily.
ⓖ The dog growled fiercely at the burglar.
ⓗ I crossed the road carefully.

Practice »

2 Write a suitable verb for each of the adverbs in the box below.
Do it like this: *quietly = to speak quietly*.

quietly	gracefully	loudly	fearlessly
politely	dangerously	generously	awkwardly

3 Copy the sentences below.
Choose a suitable adverb from the box to complete each sentence.

(a) The swans swam _____ down the river.
(b) The two children argued _____.
(c) At the back of the class they whispered _____.
(d) Raj slipped and fell _____.
(e) The man gave _____ to the charity appeal.
(f) I spoke _____ to the visitor.
(g) The tiny boy stood up to the bully _____.
(h) The police stopped the man who drove _____.

Extension »»

4 Copy and complete the chart to show three different kinds of adverbs.

Verb	When (adverb of time)	Where (adverb of place)	How (adverb of manner)
You can walk	later	here	fast
You can laugh			
You can work			
You can talk			
You can read			
You can run			
You can sing			
You can point			
You can write			

Feedback

Adverbs can often be useful to a description. For example, 'he runs' is boring. 'He runs fast' is better because the adverb describes how he ran. A strong verb is often more effective in your writing. 'He galloped' says the same thing but is better still in creating an image.

Not **all** words ending in the suffix 'ly' are adverbs: *lovely*.

Unit 5: Adjectives

Objectives ····>

- To revise work on adjectives.
- To extend the control of more complex sentences.

Grammar Focus

- **Adjectives** are **describing** words. Adjectives give us **more information about nouns**.

  A <u>strong</u> horse.

  A <u>brave</u> rider.

  An <u>exciting</u> race.

- Adjectives are used to describe nouns. They help us to make our writing and speaking more **interesting and varied**.

  The boy walked down the road is dull.

  The writer can create very different pictures by adding adjectives to create pictures in the reader's mind. This is why they are so important.

  The small boy ... enormous ... sad ... blue

  The winding road ... dusty road ... that road ... our road

Starter >

❶ Copy these sentences. Underline the adjective in each sentence. Circle the noun that it describes. The first one is done for you.

  (a) I ate a (bag of crisps) that were <u>salty</u>.
  (b) The giraffe was huge.
  (c) I put on a clean shirt.
  (d) The pencil was blunt.
  (e) The man was carrying a heavy case.
  (f) The clown wore baggy trousers.
  (g) In Autumn, leaves turn brown.
  (h) When we arrived at the park, the ground was muddy.

❷ Rewrite each of the sentences above and think of another suitable adjective to substitute.

25

Practice >>

3 Copy and complete the chart to show the variety of adjectives you can use to describe the same thing.

Noun	Shape	Size	Colour	Texture
a bee	round	tiny	black	soft
a fox				
a lion				
an elephant				
a dove				
a tortoise				
ice				
a feather				
butter				
snow				

4 Write descriptions of five of the nouns above using the adjectives you have discovered.

Extension >>>

5 'Nice' is an over-used and vague adjective. Find suitable adjectives that can be used instead of 'nice' to describe the following nouns.

(a) jacket   (c) meal   (e) holiday   (g) film
(b) book   (d) cottage   (f) day

REMEMBER

Choose adjectives with care. They can have a very powerful effect.

6 Change these nouns to adjectives by adding the same suffix. Check your spelling in a dictionary.

(a) care   (d) beauty   (g) thought   (j) doubt
(b) hope   (e) grace   (h) awe
(c) duty   (f) pity   (i) skill

Feedback ↩

Adjectives carry emotion with them. A writer can create a favourable or unfavourable image of something with the adjectives he or she chooses. For example: *The dirty, cruel boy* ... is very different from *the innocent, sad boy* ....

Objective ·····>

- To revise and extend work on pronouns.

Grammar Focus

- A **pronoun** is used **in place of a noun**. It is used to **avoid** the **repetition** of a noun in a sentence.

  <u>Fred</u> likes skating. <u>Fred</u> goes skating very day with Raj.

  <u>Fred</u> likes skating. <u>He</u> goes skating every day with Raj.

  <u>Raj</u> has new skates. <u>Raj</u> uses his new skates every day.

  <u>Raj</u> has new skates. <u>He</u> uses them every day.

Starter >

❶ Underline the pronouns in the following sentences. Circle the nouns to which they refer.

- (a) (Fred) likes skiing. <u>He</u> goes skiing every year.
- (b) Raj has new trainers and wears them every day.
- (c) The teacher loaded the software but it would not work.
- (d) Let's go to the cinema. It's very cheap.
- (e) 'Jane, get off that bike. You know you are not allowed.'
- (f) 'Tricia, Rory and Max, you can all leave school early today.'
- (g) Mr Smith ran back to his wife to tell her the story.
- (h) Mr Webb's children sat in the back of the car and all they did was laugh.
- (i) The teacher pointed at the sweets. 'Are these yours?' he asked Ann.
- (j) 'Those sweets are theirs,' cried the girl, pointing at the gang of boys.

❷ Say whether the pronouns refer to singular or plural nouns in the examples.

Practice ≫

3 Read the following article from a local newspaper.

WHALE STRANDED ON BEACH

A rare species of whale, never before seen in this country, was spotted on a Norfolk beach by an amateur rock climber.

Mr Smith from Leytonstone was climbing with friends when ___ suddenly became aware of the strange creature.

'___ was lying there stranded on the beach. ___ couldn't believe our eyes when we saw ___,' ___ said to our reporter today. '___ just stood there and watched ___, but ___ was still. ___ will never believe the excitement I felt at seeing it so close to ___. It was my first experience of a whale. ___'m looking forward to telling my wife. ___ will be so thrilled.'

___ certainly has caused a sensation in this area. ___ have all been waiting for such a wildlife scoop and we thank ___ for reporting it so promptly.

pronoun box

they	us
she	you
we	it
I	he

Now complete the passage using pronouns from the pronoun box.

Extension ≫≫≫

4 Rewrite the following sentences. Change some of the nouns to pronouns in these examples to avoid repetition.

ⓐ Dad told me he used to own a bike. Dad said he made the bike himself. Dad bought all the materials for the bike from scrapyards. Dad used the materials to make the bike. Dad did not keep the bike long. Dad sold the bike to buy a motorbike.

ⓑ It is the job of doctors to visit the sick. Doctors sometimes find it difficult to arrange times to visit the sick. Doctors require you to telephone them early in the morning if you would like the doctor to call. Doctors are under pressure. We must be helpful to doctors.

ⓒ Maz was given a new computer for her birthday. Maz also got a new game for the computer. Maz was keen to try the games. She tried the games but the games did not work. Maz called her dad. When her dad came in her dad loaded the games and the games worked straight away.

Feedback ↶

Pronouns avoid unnecessary repetition. Sometimes it is not as easy as just replacing nouns with pronouns. You have to structure your sentences in a different way as well. You also need to use the correct form of the pronoun.

Grammar Focus

There are **four main types of sentence**.

- A **question** asks something.

  What's the matter?

  A direct question needs a question mark.

- A **statement** gives information.

  I've got a headache.

  Statements are often simple sentences.

- An **exclamation** shows that the speaker feels strongly about something.

  It's all that loud music!

  An exclamation needs an exclamation mark – but only one.

- If we want someone to do something we make a **command** or a **request**.

  Go and lie down.

  Notice how the verb is a direct command in the second person. *(You) Go …*

Starter >

1 Look at the box below. Which words tell you that the sentences are questions, even though some punctuation is missing?

How much is that dog	*When can you deliver it*
Which one	*Where to*
Why do you want to know	*Who will be home*

2 Punctuate each of the questions above correctly.

3 Match up the questions and the statements in this chart.

Questions	Statements
Where is my pen?	*Victoria was a famous queen.*
What is the capital of France?	*I kicked a ball through the glass.*
Who was Victoria?	*Your pen is on the table.*
When was the French Revolution?	*I am going swimming.*
How did you break the window?	*It started in 1789.*
Why are you carrying a towel?	*Paris is the capital of France.*

Practice >>

4 The following instructions consist of commands.
They are not in the correct order. Rewrite them correctly.

- Get in the bath.
- Get out of the bath.
- Dry yourself with a towel.
- Take off your clothes.
- Put in the plug.
- Get dressed.
- Fill the bath with water.
- Have a thorough wash.

5 Look at your rewritten sentences from question 4.
Underline the verbs which show us that these are commands.

6 Rewrite the instructions as a set of statements as if you had carried
them out. Do it like this:

I put in the plug and filled the bath with water. Then I ...

Extension >>>

7 Copy these sentences. After each, write if it is a
statement (S), a question (Q), a command (C)
or an exclamation (E). Explain how you know.

(a) What happened to my CD?
(b) What a nightmare that was!
(c) Look at the state you're in!
(d) I have been playing on my skateboard.
(e) Go and clean yourself up.
(f) It's not fair.
(g) Don't tell lies.
(h) That's fantastic!

8 Write a conversation between two
people using each of the four kinds of
sentence.

REMEMBER

Each different
kind of sentence
needs its own
special
punctuation.

Feedback ↩

- Direct questions need question marks.
- Exclamations need exclamation marks.
  Avoid using too many exclamation
  marks as this lessens the impact of the
  strong feeling being expressed.
- Different kinds of sentences have their
  own grammar rules. For example,
  commands use the second person of the
  verb: *(You) Stop that!*

Objectives ····>

- To re-order simple sentences.
- To extend the control of more complex sentences.

Grammar Focus

- A **sentence** should **make sense on its own**. It should begin with a capital letter. Most sentences end with a full stop.

  The dog chased the postman. This is a sentence.

  The dog. This is **not** a sentence.

- Sentences which contain one piece of information (a clause) are called **simple sentences**.

- A **clause** is a group of words. It must contain a **verb** and have a **subject**.

  James ran home.

  In the **one-clause sentence** above, James is the **subject**, ran is the **verb**.

- When simple **sentences** are joined together, they make **compound sentences**. Both clauses are equally important.

  The dog chased the postman. The postman could run faster. Two **simple** sentences.

  The dog chased the postman, but the postman could run faster. One **compound** sentence.

Starter >

❶ The words in these sentences are jumbled up. Rewrite them in the correct order to make simple sentences.

- (a) looked a gloomy Treasure Island place
- (b) were wooded The lower parts
- (c) I hated Even the thought in the sunshine of it
- (d) anchored in an were inlet We
- (e) Trees down water to the came
- (f) air still was The
- (g) The restless men were
- (h) to Captain the gave men ashore Smollett leave go

Practice ≫

② The box below contains common conjunctions that are used to make compound sentences.

Conjunction box			
and	but	or	so

Combine the simple sentences to make compound sentences. Use the conjunctions to help. Write out your new sentences.

(a) Fred hesitated. Then he spoke.
(b) The clouds were thinner. It became sunnier.
(c) A helicopter came into view. They began to hope.
(d) I like Christmas cake. I like Easter eggs better.
(e) The miser is very rich. He is very mean.
(f) Mario's father lives in Manchester. He sometimes lives in Rome.
(g) It is boiling hot in the desert during the day. It is freezing at night.
(h) They might go on holiday to France. They might go to Italy.

Extension ≫≫

❸ Combine some of the simple sentences in this passage to make more interesting ones.

> The rocket dropped into the clouds. The clouds were dense. They were a few kilometers from the surface. The rocket gave a shudder. It crashed. It came to rest at a dangerous angle. Its tail fin was broken.

❹ A character called Mr Jingle in a novel by Charles Dickens speaks in a very strange way. Rewrite the passage in sentences.

> "Heads, heads – take care of your heads," cried the stranger. "Terrible place – dangerous – other day – five children – mother – tall lady – eating sandwiches – forgot the arch – crash – knock – children look around – mother's head off – sandwich in her hand – no mouth to put it in."

Feedback ↩

Here are some ways to make sentences more interesting. Discuss the impact of each one.

- Begin with a connective: *Meanwhile, we all sat and waited.*
- Begin with a word ending in 'ing': *Sitting quietly, we all waited.*

Objectives ••••>

- To construct sentences in different ways.
- To extend the control of more complex sentences.

Grammar Focus

- A **phrase** usually consists of two or more words. It **cannot make sense by itself** as it does **not** have a **verb**.

  The fog crept <u>through the streets</u>.

  'Through the streets' is a phrase.

- Adding phrases is a way of making sentences more interesting.

  I walked down the road.

  How did you walk?

  I walked down the road <u>as fast as possible</u>.

Starter >

❶ Copy the sentences.
Underline the phrases in each.
The first one is done for you.

  (a) Amit followed <u>in his father's footsteps</u>.
  (b) The jet plane passed like a flash of lightning.
  (c) Her jumper was embroidered with cartoon cats.
  (d) My mum shouted loudly at the dog.
  (e) The football crowd cheered at the second goal.
  (f) Most policemen wear uniform except when on plain clothes duty.
  (g) Jane's daughter was taken to hospital after the accident.
  (h) Fred's mum said goodbye at the corner of the street.

Practice »

❷ Write full sentences using a phrase from column A, a verb from column B and a phrase from column C.
Gardeners say that <u>black flowers</u> <u>are</u> <u>impossible to grow</u>.
You may need to change the form of the verb.

Column A	Column B	Column C
ⓐ black flowers	seem	a long time away
ⓑ summer holidays	pollute	the atmosphere of restaurants
ⓒ Christmas Day	occur	up and down our street
ⓓ the driver	say	impossible to grow
ⓔ my mum	are	arguments between husbands and wives
ⓕ learning to drive	zoom	on the 25th of December
ⓖ the sun	cause	out to work
ⓗ many sunbathers	heat	the soil in our garden
ⓘ smokers	go	ill later in life

Extension »»

❸ Phrases can give more information about a noun:
The clown <u>with a bright red nose</u>.
Or they can give information about a **verb**:
He was standing <u>waist high in the water</u>.
Write these phrases in sentences of your own.

ⓐ with a bright red cherry on top
ⓑ by the side of the deep river
ⓒ at the top of a tall tree

❹ Make up your own phrases to describe the nouns below.

ⓐ a dog   ⓓ a cathedral
ⓑ a book   ⓔ a grandfather clock
ⓒ a wasp

❺ Write the phrases in sentences. For example:
The clown <u>with a bright red nose</u> made me laugh.

REMEMBER

Phrases are <u>not</u> sentences. Sentences have a verb – <u>phrases do not</u>.

Feedback ↻

Phrases should be used to add extra meaning to a sentence. They make your sentences longer and more interesting.

Objectives ••••>

- To investigate adjectival phrases.
- To extend the control of more complex sentences.

Grammar Focus 📁

- A **phrase** is a group of words.
- A phrase is usually **short** and does **not** have a **verb**.
- A phrase does **not make sense on its own**.
- Look at the sentence below.

  The girl <u>with the curly hair</u> was the winner.

  This phrase tells us more about the noun 'girl'.

  It does the job of an adjective.

  It is called an **adjectival phrase**.

Starter >

❶ Consider each of the phrases in the phrase box. Explain why they are phrases.

> **Phrase box**
>
> *soft and white*   *crowded and noisy*
> *burning hot*   *slippery and icy*
> *messy and dirty*

❷ Copy the sentences below. Choose the best adjectival phrase from the phrase box to complete each sentence.

  ⓐ My bedroom was _____.
  ⓑ The sun was _____.
  ⓒ The shop was _____.
  ⓓ In the winter the street was _____.
  ⓔ The rabbit's tail was _____.

Practice ≫

3 Copy sentences (a) to (h).
Choose the best adjectival phrase from the box and complete each one.

> dirty but happy, rocky and snowy, muddy and battered,
> with the torn corner, dark and handsome, in the black anorak,
> neat and tidy, long and tangled

(a) The prince was _____.
(b) Her garden was _____.
(c) In the 'before' advert her hair was _____.
(d) The two children were _____ when they came home from the park.
(e) My _____ car was returned by the police.
(f) The mountain looked _____.
(g) The thief _____ came in.
(h) My library book, _____, was found under the chair.

4 Use the same sentences above. Complete them by using some different adjectival phrases of your own.

Extension ≫≫

5 Describe the nouns in (a) to (f).
See how long you can make your description without using a verb. Look at the example to see how to do it.

> The cake – the chocolate cake – the big chocolate cake – the big chocolate cake with icing – the big chocolate cake with icing and cherries on the top – the big chocolate cake with icing and cherries on top on a silver dish ...

(a) the car
(b) the garden
(c) the spacecraft
(d) the alien
(e) the carpet
(f) the teacher

Feedback ↩

Phrases should be used to add extra meaning to sentences. They make your sentences longer and more interesting.

Improve your writing by using adjectival phrases to extend your sentences.

Unit 11: Clauses

Objective ·····>

- To investigate clauses.

Grammar Focus

- A **clause** is a group of words. It can be used as a **whole** sentence or a **part** of a sentence. It contains a **verb** and usually has a **subject**.

Tracey walked home.

In the **one-clause sentence** above, Tracey is the **subject**, walked is the **verb**.

- The sentence below contains **two** clauses.

Tracey walked home   but   Emma caught the bus.

(clause 1)   (clause 2)

Note that **each** clause has a subject and a verb. They are connected by the word 'but'.

Starter >

❶ Copy these one-clause sentences.
Underline the subject in each.
Circle the verb or verbs.
The first one is done for you.

- ⓐ Trevor (helped) at the church.
- ⓑ We cannot buy a ticket.
- ⓒ The shop assistant got the sack.
- ⓓ You can wait until later.
- ⓔ John, please put that cake back in the tin.
- ⓕ I like going to Portugal.
- ⓖ They sheltered in the museum.
- ⓗ The football player was injured.

Practice >>

❷ Copy these sentences. Underline the verbs and say if each sentence contains one or two clauses.

ⓐ We will be going to the disco.
ⓑ My hair turned bright orange after I used my sister's shampoo.
ⓒ You should take the antibiotics so that the infection will be killed.
ⓓ Maz was starving after the match.
ⓔ My mum tied up the tree branch after the storm had blown it down.
ⓕ She was desperate for a drink of water.
ⓖ The racing driver turned fast into the final bend so that he could overtake the World Champion.
ⓗ I left a trail of paper in the maze.
ⓘ I kicked the ball towards the goal.
ⓙ Although we were only playing a friendly game, the opposing team decided to beat us.

❸ Circle the word used to connect the clauses in the two-clause sentences above.

Extension >>>

❹ Add clauses beginning with 'because' or 'if' to these sentences. Do it like this:

I will not give her a ticket because she still owes me money.

ⓐ We will not be going out this morning ...
ⓑ My nose turned a bright red colour ...
ⓒ The football team shook hands and embraced ...
ⓓ People started to eat at the pavement cafés ...
ⓔ I decided to buy the trainers ...
ⓕ The conductor will have to stop the performance …
ⓖ I will be top of the class again this year ...
ⓗ The headteacher is certain to lose her temper ...

REMEMBER

Clauses add extra meaning and interest to sentences.

❺ Turn the sentence around to make it more interesting.

Because she still owes me money, I will not give her a ticket.

Feedback ↩

A clause can be used as a whole sentence if it makes sense on its own. You join two clauses together using 'joining words' such as connectives or conjunctions.

Objective ·····>

- To revise work on complex sentences.

Grammar Focus

- Every **simple sentence** must contain **one clause**. A simple sentence **makes sense on its own**.

  Pinocchio's nose grew bigger.

- **Complex sentences** contain a **main clause** and another, **less important clause**. The less important (**subordinate**) clause does **not make sense by itself**. The subordinate clause depends on the main clause for meaning.

  Pinocchio's nose grew bigger <u>as he told more lies</u>.

- There are various ways to add detail to sentences.

  You could use 'who' to join two clauses if you are talking about a person.

  Mark Twain, who wrote 'Huckleberry Finn', was American.

  You could use 'which' to join two clauses if you are talking about a place or a thing.

  The Nile, which is in Egypt, is the longest river in Africa.

Starter >

❶ Copy the sentences.
Circle the main clause in each sentence.
Underline the subordinate clause.
The first one is done for you.

  ⓐ (The fisherman caught a pike) <u>after he waited for an hour</u>.
  ⓑ He scored the goal when the keeper fell to the ground.
  ⓒ The red car shot round the corner before it crashed into the tree.
  ⓓ John's jacket was cheap although it looked expensive.
  ⓔ I will not go out tonight because I have a headache.
  ⓕ Because I do not like her, I will not share my lunch.
  ⓖ If I go to the film, I will sit by myself.

Practice »

2 Join each pair of sentences using the pronoun 'who':
Dickens wrote 'Oliver Twist'. He was a famous novelist.
Dickens, <u>who</u> wrote 'Oliver Twist', was a famous novelist.

(a) Charlie Chaplin was a famous comedian. He died some years ago.
(b) The Italian used to play for an English team. He now manages a French team.
(c) Robin Hood lived in Nottingham. He robbed the rich to give to the poor.
(d) My mum is a great mechanic. She owns the garage around the corner.
(e) John Lennon was a member of the Beatles. He came from Liverpool.

3 Join each pair of sentences using the pronoun 'which':
Fred's bike is very expensive. It comes from France.
Fred's bike, <u>which</u> is very expensive, comes from France.

(a) The table is an antique. It is two hundred years old.
(b) The football match was between two London teams. It ended after the first goal.
(c) Fresh strawberries are good for the skin. They are not always available.
(d) The Rocky Mountains are parallel to the coast. They get most of the rain on the West coast.
(e) The police force was founded by Robert Peel. It celebrated its anniversary recently.

Extension »»

4 Join these pairs of sentences using suitable connectives. Write each example as one sentence.

(a) No one will leave the class. The headteacher has made her choice.
(b) You need to learn to swim. You can perform lifesaving.
(c) His father bought him a new computer. He should have waited for the sales.
(d) My cousin was very confident. He did not pass the exam.
(e) Drive for an hour. You pass an old church with a steeple.
(f) He poured water over my head. I was soaked.
(g) My father cannot give you any money. He would like to be helpful.
(h) My bedroom was very untidy. I decided to tidy it up.

> **REMEMBER**
>
> Use a variety of simple and complex sentences to make your written work more interesting.

> **Feedback** ↩
>
> A subordinate clause adds extra detail to a sentence. You can use 'who' or 'which' to join clauses. There are many other connectives you can use to introduce subordinate clauses, such as 'after', 'although', 'when', 'if', 'that'.

Unit 13: Active and passive verbs

Objective ·····>

- To use the active or the passive voice to suit purpose.

Grammar Focus

- A verb is in the **active** 'voice' when the **subject** of the verb is actually **performing the action** of the sentence.

  Fred drove the new, red car.

  Fred is the subject of the sentence. He is the one performing the action. He is driving the car.

- A verb is **passive** when the action of the verb is **being done to the subject by someone** or **something else** in the sentence. It uses verbs such as 'was' and 'were'.

  The car was driven by Fred.

  The car is the subject of the sentence. The verb 'to drive' applies to the car and not to Fred.

Starter >

❶ Copy the sentences. Underline the active verbs and circle the subject of each sentence. The first one is done for you.

   (a) (The wind) <u>blew</u> strongly all night.
   (b) His appearance took me by surprise.
   (c) Suddenly, the door flew open.
   (d) My uncle grew the prize-winning tomatoes at the Show.
   (e) Shoppers crowded the streets in their rush to buy Christmas gifts.

❷ Copy the sentences. Underline the passive verbs and circle the subject of each sentence. The first one is done for you.

   (a) (The plate) <u>was dropped</u> by my brother.
   (b) The robber was taken by surprise by the owner of the house.
   (c) All the sweets were eaten by the children.
   (d) Several books wcrc thrown out of the bus by the girls.
   (e) Some jewellery is being examined by the police for fingerprints.

Practice >>

3 Copy the sentences. Underline the verbs.
Rewrite the sentences. Change the passive verb to an active one:

The car <u>was driven</u> by the priest. The priest <u>drove</u> the car.

(a) My luggage is being inspected by a customs officer.
(b) The garage doors are operated by two guards.
(c) I was guided to my seat by a young lady.
(d) In our school nursery children are looked after by Mrs Randall.
(e) The glass was dropped by Robert.

4 Copy the sentences. Underline the verbs.
Rewrite the sentences. Change the active verb to a passive one:

The priest <u>drove</u> the car. The car <u>was driven</u> by the priest.

(a) Thick, wool carpets deadened the noise in the hall.
(b) CD radios direct the police to the crime.
(c) In the store, glass lifts take customers to the top floor.
(d) Our workshops carry out all kinds of car repairs.
(e) Bad storms delayed the arrival of Concorde.

Extension >>>

5 Rewrite this experiment, using only active verbs.

The test tube was taken by the teacher and was placed in the flame. It was then heated until some bubbles in the water were seen. We were told by Miss Sunhilla to keep out of the way as it might be dangerous. The temperature of the liquid was taken by the teacher and was recorded in the chart. Then the liquid was left in a cold place in the classroom until it was seen to change colour. While this was happening the white solid was heated in another part of the room. When this was seen to change colour also and to give off a gas, the liquid and the solid were mixed together. Finally the test tube was washed out and was returned carefully to the shelf. By the time this had happened, small blue crystals were seen to form. We were asked to watch them until they grew to a large size. When the experiment was completed we were allowed to hang the pretty crystals in the class.

Feedback ↩

Use of the active and passive voice varies in different types of text. For example, experiments are written in the passive because it is not usually important to know who performed the action in an experiment.

Unit 14: Ambiguity

Objective ·····>

- To recognise and remedy ambiguity in sentences.

Grammar Focus

- Words are **ambiguous** when they can have **more than one meaning**.
- Often ambiguous phrases are funny, like this newspaper headline:

BOY HITS GIRL WITH ICE CREAM

Is the girl hit with an ice cream by a boy?

Is the girl carrying an ice cream when she is hit?

- Be careful not to split an adverb from the verb it qualifies.

He needed his teeth cleaning badly is ambiguous.

He badly needed to clean his teeth is clearer.

Starter >

❶ For each of the following words write two sentences to show that the word can have more than one meaning. Use the clues in brackets. The first one is done for you.

(a) match (fire, football) – We went to the football match.
The match went out in the rain.

(b) ball (round, dancing)
(c) date (diary, fruit)
(d) bank (money, high slope)
(e) sole (foot, fish)
(f) fire (flames, an arrow)
(g) ruler (measure, King)

❷ Each of the words below has at least two different meanings. Explain two meanings by using the words in sentences.

pine, pitch, junk, mine, pole

Practice >>

3 Explain what is ambiguous in each of these sentences. Use the clues in brackets.

(a) The scientist showed me his cure for spots on the nose, which he developed after five years' research. (What did he develop?)

(b) My friend Tracy told Maria that she was a nuisance. (Who was a nuisance?)

(c) I collected worms from the garden where they lived on Sunday. (Where did the worms live for the rest of the week?)

(d) Did you see that fascinating programme about sleeping on your television? (Were you really snoring on top of the TV?)

(e) Ahmed enjoyed visiting museums more than his friends. (Did he really not like his friends that much?)

(f) The squirrel picked up the nut and after breaking the shell on a large rock, ate it. (What did the squirrel eat?)

(g) When I met the artist I told him that I painted myself in my spare time. (Did I really paint my body?)

4 Write versions of these sentences so they only have one meaning.

Extension >>>

5 Write each example below again so that the meaning is clear.
Explain the two meanings they could have.

(a) Do you get headaches? You need to go and have your eyes examined to cure them.

(b) Make sure all medicines are put away safely. If there are children in the house, put them in a cabinet that locks.

(c) Try feeding your baby with fresh milk. If the baby does not get on well with this, it should be boiled for five minutes.

(d) He came upon a van full of chickens that had broken down.

(e) REPORTER FINDS FATHER OF TWELVE.

REMEMBER

Usually, when you read something aloud, your mistakes become obvious!

Feedback ↻

Some causes of ambiguity in writing are:

- an unclear use of pronouns. The reader needs to know who is being referred to in a sentence
- changing person in the middle of a sentence – from third to first person.

Keep the parts of a sentence that talk about the same thing together.

Objective ·····>

- To recognise how commas, connectives and full stops are used to join and separate clauses.

Grammar Focus

- These two sentences are **separated** by a **full stop**.

  Simon was feeling bored. He went home.

- These two statements are connected by a **conjunction** (the joining word 'so').

  Simon was feeling bored so he went home.

- The **word order** has been **changed** and a **new word** (as) has been **added**. A **comma** has been used to join the sentences together.

  As he was feeling bored, Simon went home.

Starter >

❶ Make the pairs of sentences below into one sentence. Choose the best conjunction to help you.

ⓐ The lady put up her umbrella. It was raining. (because, and, but)

ⓑ I tried hard. I could not do it. (and, so, but)

ⓒ The man sat down. He watched television. (if, although, when)

ⓓ I hurt my leg. I was playing football. (after, and, when)

ⓔ The car is useless. It is broken. (but, while, because)

ⓕ I asked John to come. He refused. (and, so, but)

ⓖ Mrs Jones will go shopping. It does not rain. (if, so, because)

ⓗ Tom waved to Sam. She did not see him. (and, when, but)

❷ Discuss some of the differences in meaning that can be achieved by using different conjunctions. Do it like this:

'Because' suggests a cause and effect.
'And' simply joins and continues the idea.
'But' suggests an alternative.

Practice >>

❸ Rewrite each sentence below as two shorter sentences.

(a) Jock could not lift the box because it was too heavy.

(b) I went to the window and looked out.

(c) As it was late, Edward went to bed.

(d) When Tom told a lie, his mother was very angry.

(e) That is the girl who lost her bag.

(f) We walked across the road which ran through town.

(g) It rained heavily so I got soaked.

(h) I read my book while Emma watched television.

Extension >>>

❹ Copy the sentences below. Put in the missing commas.

(a) After the police captured the thief they handcuffed him.

(b) Because he was ill Tom could not go out.

(c) While she was walking along Amy tripped and fell.

(d) Tom wondering what to do walked along the road.

(e) As I waited for the bus I whistled to myself.

(f) The rabbit which was only young came out of the burrow.

(g) Although the sky was cloudy we could still see the moon.

(h) Mr Barnes who is my next door neighbour threw my ball back.

❺ Now rewrite each of the sentences as two shorter sentences.

Feedback ↩

If you know how to separate sentences you will be able to vary your writing to achieve the effect you want.

In the past, writers tended to write long, carefully structured sentences. Now, sentences tend to be much shorter and more direct. Short sentences can be used to create a sense of drama; longer sentences can be used to suggest a tired, ever moving effect.

Objective ·····>

- To use punctuation effectively to signpost meaning.

Grammar Focus 📁

- Just a few **punctuation marks** can make a great **difference to meaning**.

> **DANGER**
> **NO SWIMMING ALLOWED**

This makes the situation sound dangerous.

> **DANGER?**
> **NO. SWIMMING ALLOWED.**

This makes the situation safe.

Starter >

❶ Write out two sentences and clauses as a single sentence. Punctuate them correctly.

She'll buy a new pair of jeans. If she can find some to fit her.
She'll buy a new pair of jeans, if she can find some to fit her.

(a) He kept on laughing. Although the teacher kept telling him off.

(b) She is an attractive dog. Though she has no tail.

(c) He used to be in a rock band. Before which he was a dustman.

(d) Maggie is going to college. Unless she gets married.

(e) We are having insulation put in our loft. In case the winter is a cold one.

(f) We are going to Spain for our holidays. Provided we can save the money.

(g) Everybody ought to have a pet. Because it relaxes you and makes you more caring.

Practice >>

② Write out the notice below. Put in an exclamation mark, a question mark or a full stop where there is ___ to make it mean the opposite.

QUEUE HERE   QUEUE HERE___
NO PUSHING ALLOWED   NO___ PUSHING ALLOWED___

How does the meaning change?

③ Punctuate these two pieces of speech so as to make their meaning clear.

ⓐ Are you all ready Right off we go
ⓑ Is that car yours Trevor thats fantastic

④ Punctuate this sentence in a different way to change its meaning.
Eat this boy.
(Are you a cannibal or are you pointing at something to eat?)

Extension >>>

⑤ Write out the poems again.
Punctuate them so that they make sense.
There is more than one way of doing this.

ⓐ Every lady in the land
Has twenty nails on each hand
Five and twenty on hands and feet
And this is true without deceit

ⓑ Caesar entered on his head
A helmet on each foot
A sandal in his hand he had
His trusty sword to boot

REMEMBER
Clear punctuation makes it easier for the reader to work out the meaning.

Feedback ↩

It is vital that appropriate punctuation is used if people are to understand what we have written.

Punctuation can also change meaning as the examples in this unit prove.

The best way to check if your punctuation makes sense is to ask someone else to read your work. It soon becomes evident if the punctuation you have used is accurate.

Objective ·····⟩

• To use speech punctuation accurately.

Grammar Focus 📁

• We use **speech marks** when we write down what people actually say.

• Only the words actually spoken – the **direct speech** – go inside the speech marks.

   'What's the problem?' the mechanic asked.

   The man replied, 'The engine won't start.'

• When someone new speaks, always begin a new line.

   If you introduce speech, use a comma.

   The driver said, 'I can see that the engine won't start.'

• Before you close the speech marks and use verbs such as 'said', use a comma.

   'I can see that the engine won't start,' said the driver.

• Punctuation marks used in the speech should go inside the speech marks.

   'What do you expect me to do?' asked the mechanic.

Starter ⟩

❶ Underline the actual words spoken in each of these sentences. The first one is done for you.

   ⓐ Edward said, <u>It must be my turn next</u>.
   ⓑ I like skating best of all, said Shahidi.
   ⓒ Asif said, There is a great new sports shop in town.
   ⓓ My favourite team is Liverpool, Kim said.
   ⓔ Mrs Merton said, I hate cabbage!
   ⓕ Have you ever slept in a haunted house? James said.
   ⓖ It's not fair! Nasi said.
   ⓗ My homework is better than yours, Raza said.

❷ Rewrite the sentences. Put in the missing speech marks.

❸ Each of these sentences uses the verb 'said' to describe the way the people spoke the words. Using a thesaurus find more accurate and interesting verbs to use. For example:
   James 'asked' a question
   Raza 'boasted'.

Practice >>

4 Rewrite the sentences. Put in all the missing punctuation.

ⓐ please will you lend me your library ticket sam asked
ⓑ the lady said the red trainers are the smartest
ⓒ stop that at once shouted the angry teacher
ⓓ those new games cost three pounds the assistant explained.
ⓔ i can't find my new jacket the boy cried
ⓕ where do you think you are going at this time of night the policeman asked
ⓖ i'm dying for a drink leo groaned so let's go in here and get one
ⓗ please show me what new books you have the man requested but not anything too expensive

Extension >>>

5 Write this short play in sentence form using appropriate speech marks. You can add detail to make the dialogue more interesting. Do it like this: *'Mum, I'm starving,' pleaded Shireen, rubbing her stomach.*

Shireen: Mum, I'm starving.
Mum: Not again? You've only just eaten.
Shireen: Come on, mum. I'm desperate for some chocolate.
Mum: No. You've done nothing but stuff your face all day. You'll be the size of a house if you're not careful.
Shireen: That's not fair, mum. You eat all the time. I don't moan about you smoking, do I?
Mum: That's got nothing to do with it. Smoking is my business and does not affect you.
Shireen: Oh yes it does. I inhale as much smoke as you when you're in this room. My eating is far healthier.
Mum: If you're that keen on health, have an apple.

6 Continue the conversation between the two characters in play form. Then rewrite the same dialogue as direct speech.

Feedback ↶

Use these questions to help check your punctuation:
• Are the actual words spoken in speech marks?
• Have you used a new line for each new speaker?
• Is your punctuation inside the speech marks?

Objectives ····>

- To recognise the cues to start new paragraphs.
- To identify the main point in a paragraph.

Grammar Focus

- A **paragraph** is a **group of sentences** about **one** particular **subject**. The sentences in a paragraph should be linked in some way because they should all be about the **same idea**.

- The **main sentence** in a paragraph is called the **topic sentence**.

- Every **new idea** needs a **new paragraph**.

- Paragraphs help us because they break up the text into smaller, more readable parts.

- Here are some points to help you remember when to begin a new paragraph:

  – a change of time

  – a change of speaker

  – a change of place

  – a change of topic

  – a new point being made.

Starter >

1 Read the passage below which has not been divided into paragraphs.

> Milk is made up mainly of water but it contains nearly all the food types required by human beings. Hence it is given to babies. It looks white in a glass because it contains casein – a protein. If you look at milk through a microscope you can see blobs of fat floating around. In fact this is what makes the cream on the top of milk. Besides casein and fat, milk contains a sugar, called lactose, which we cannot see. You can also find calcium and phosphorus in milk, essential for building healthy bones and teeth. We all know that milk is produced by female mammals to feed their young. All mammals – even whales – suckle from their mothers for milk. Man has realised the value of milk for children for centuries and so cows and other milk-bearing animals have been kept for farming use. You can even find buffaloes milked in certain eastern countries!

Decide where three new paragraphs should go.
Explain the clues that tell you this.

Practice >>

2 In the following two paragraphs the sentences are in the wrong order. Rewrite each paragraph as a continuous, correctly ordered, paragraph. Explain how you know what order they should be in.

> Joseph's younger brother had two children called Tracey and Maria. This means that Mike's aunt and cousin had the same name.
> Joseph had two children.
> Mike was the elder.
> Mike's grandfather had three sons and one daughter.
> The eldest son was called Joseph and the daughter Tracey.

> Decorate the edges with the back of a fork.
> Place the dough shapes on a greased baking tray.
> Bake in an oven at Gas mark 4 for half an hour.
> Mix the flour, salt and water.
> Shape the dough into circles or triangles.
> Leave overnight.
> Knead well for five minutes.
> Eat the bread!

> **REMEMBER**
>
> Each paragraph should be about a new idea and should have a topic, or main, sentence.

Extension >>>

3 Copy these paragraphs. Underline the topic sentence in each.

> Those were the days of the boiling hot summers. Our street would be hot, airless and dirty. All the curtains would be drawn and the blinds down. The paving stones were so hot you could fry eggs, and the dust hung in the air. Silence reigned.

> When the first Americans went to their new country they had to find words to describe new things. They borrowed words from native Americans such as 'skunk', 'moccasin' and 'totem'. As the US became more prosperous, new influences arose there. Jazz gave us a whole new vocabulary and 'the movies' still give us new words. So, one of the main additions to our language has been American English.

4 List each of the points made to illustrate the theme in each paragraph above.

5 Write a short paragraph on one of the following, incorporating a topic sentence.

ⓐ a day in winter
ⓑ how your language is influenced by TV

> **Feedback** ↩
>
> Paragraphs are important because they help us to divide up our written work so that it can be more easily read and the content understood.

Unit 19: Main points

Objectives ••••>

- To identify the main point in a paragraph.
- To recognise how sentences are organised in a paragraph.

Grammar Focus

- A **paragraph** is a **group of sentences** about **one particular subject**.

- Paragraphs should contain one clearly stated idea, called the **topic sentence**. This is the key to understanding what the paragraph is about.

- The topic sentence will make a **general statement** and the rest of the paragraph will illustrate this.

- The sentences in a particular paragraph need to be **organised carefully** to make maximum sense.

- When the **subject changes**, begin a **new paragraph**.

- Try and organise the information in your paragraphs logically.

- Most paragraphs contain material in a chronological order.

Starter >

❶ Read this paragraph and say what is wrong with it.

When I was eight I was given a mountain bike for Christmas. It had big, fat, black tyres, a great saddle and a flashy set of gears. Isn't it strange that I can still remember that? My friend kept on borrowing it. I remember once one of my brother's friends took it for a day and I thought it had been stolen. He was in the rugby team. I don't much like people borrowing my things without asking. My girlfriend is a bit like that now so I suppose I can't get away from it. She keeps borrowing my car without telling me and I've called the police twice to report it missing. I wish I could afford to buy her one this Christmas. Now if she needed a bike that would be different.

❷ Rewrite the paragraph, adding and changing information, to make it more logical and interesting.

Practice »

3 Copy these paragraphs. Underline the topic sentence in each.

> The ship was ready to leave. A puff of smoke and a hooter blaring warned the passengers. Sailors hurried about casting off huge ropes. Passengers hung over the rails waving frantically. The captain announced a farewell, blew the horn again and we could feel the huge propeller turning. We were on our way.

> First you have to pump up the tyres. Then you need to check the oil and make sure the lights are all functioning correctly. If you are travelling to Europe you may even have to buy special yellow filters. Insurance cover for overseas is essential in case you have an accident. These are just some of the things you need to do before you take your car abroad.

4 Choose one of the paragraphs above. List each of the points made to illustrate the main theme of the paragraph.

5 Write a short paragraph on one of the following.

(a) Saying goodbye to someone at a station.
(b) Instructing a friend on how to buy a new skateboard.
(c) How to get tickets for the Cup Final.

Extension »»

6 Use the following sequence of events to structure and write a paragraph:

> Twelve o'clock – midnight – no moon – the graveyard by the ruined church – spooky noises – shadows – strange figure looms   so what did you do?

REMEMBER

If you change subject, start a new paragraph with a new topic sentence.

7 These events are not in the correct sequence. Correct the sequence and write the paragraph.

> You knock – An old caravan – A storm at night – You go in – You shout – You need to shelter – Nothing happens – So, what is in there?

Feedback ↻

Paragraphs help break up your work into smaller 'chunks' of information. Topic sentences often come at the beginning of a paragraph – but they don't have to.

41

Unit 20: Paragraph structure

Objectives ····>

- To recognise how sentences are organised in a paragraph.
- To vary the structure of sentences in a paragraph.
- To organise ideas in a paragraph.

Grammar Focus

- Paragraphs should not just be a jumble of ideas written in a block. When we organise ideas in a paragraph we need to **sequence** the ideas in a sensible order. This is important so that your reader can follow logically what you are trying to say.

- Many paragraphs contain ideas that are presented in **chronological** (time) order. This is essential for texts such as recipes, instructions and stories.

- The words that you use to link ideas in a paragraph are important.

Starter >

❶ Read the arguments against smoking.

> Costs £100 million a year. Thousands of hospital beds used up. Causes young people to give in to peer pressure. Young people waste money. Stops young people playing sport. Creates black market in cigarettes. Cause of ill health – not just lungs but heart. Passive smoking – we all take in the smoke. 80% of cigarette smoke gets into the air. Leads to acceptance of drugs.

❷ Copy and complete the chart with these arguments.

Financial issues	Health issues	Social issues

❸ Write a paragraph for each issue using this information. Start each sentence in a different way.

Practice »

4 Read the notes about the derivation of surnames.

Use them as the basis for writing three paragraphs.

Think carefully about how you will start your sentences and how you will vary them.

Derivation of surnames	Geographical names	Occupational names
No-one had surnames before 1066 – first records – how to distinguish people. 'surname': *sur* = over and above.	First names showed where people lived – John by the river – John River: kind of address – also Hill, Dale, Woods.	Names show what people do – act as label: Thatcher, Tyler, Smith, Hunter.

5 Make up another paragraph about famous people's names.

Extension »»

6 Here is a plan for a piece of written work on 'My Favourite TV Programme'.

Paragraph 1   My preferences. Sorts of programme I like. The programme I like best.
Paragraph 2   What it's about. The story.
Paragraph 3   Characters. The ones I like and dislike and why.
Paragraph 4   My favourite episode.
Paragraph 5   Why it's better than others. Why it's different.
Paragraph 6   The future of the programme. How it will develop.

- Give your piece of written work a title.
- Make notes for each paragraph.
- Think of a topic sentence for each paragraph.
- Organise the relevant details for each paragraph.
- Think of how you will connect the sentences in each paragraph; use words from the box to help.

> *First of all, therefore, at first, so, then, however, also*

Feedback ↩

The main point in a paragraph is often supported by further information and supporting details or some comment by the author.

The best way to know if you are writing in correct and interesting paragraphs is to ask someone else to read your work and comment on it.

Unit 21: Sentence variety

Objectives ····>
- To use connectives to link clauses and sentences.
- To use and control complex sentences.

Grammar Focus

- **Connectives** are words and phrases which can **join together ideas**.

  I will teach you a lesson <u>as soon as</u> I can get out of this river.

- You should consider how you can construct sentences in different ways to vary them.

  – You could re-order the clauses.

  I liked the story of the film although the acting was awful.

  Although the acting was awful, I liked the story of the film.

  – You could put more information in the middle of your sentence inside commas.

  The bee, almost dropping with exhaustion, reached the hive.

  – You could start with an action.

  Jumping in, she held her breath.

Starter >

1 Copy the sentences.
Circle the connectives.
Underline the ideas they join. The first one is done for you.

(a) <u>She slept through the film</u> (while) <u>her baby sister crawled into the garden</u>.

(b) You will get no pocket money this week unless you start to clean your room.

(c) I liked the story of the film although the acting was awful.

(d) This trip will cost £200 today whereas it could cost twice as much tomorrow.

(e) I never go to that gym to train because it costs too much.

(f) She worked hard every night for a month in order to come first in the exams.

(g) Jan saved up for a year so that she could buy a new computer.

(h) You will only stand a chance in the lottery if you buy a ticket.

2 Discuss how the choice of connective has influenced the meaning of each sentence above. For example, 'because' seems to suggest one part of the sentence is a result of the other.

Practice >>

3 Look at the connectives in the box below.

as long as	since	until	however
on the other hand	consequently	therefore	

Now join the simple sentences from Column A to an idea from Column B using a connective from the box.

Column A	Column B
(a) Smoking is bad for you	he didn't stay with her.
(b) The bird pulled on the worm	where would people get educated?
(c) Lee would not take skiing lessons	I started going to the gym.
(d) Mike refused to take his medicine	he broke his leg in the snow.
(e) I used to be a weakling	he never got well.
(f) I believe that school should be banned	the worm would not budge.
(g) Sheila said she would go with him	nicotine is a poison.

Write out the sentences.

Extension >>>

4 Write out this passage. Join some of the sentences by using connectives.

Before 1066 no-one had a surname. There was no need for them. Few people could read. The population was so small. Everyone knew local people. They lived in his or her village. Written records were needed. People needed names. Surname means 'extra name'. By 1500 everyone had a surname. It was normal. Some people were named after their jobs. Blacksmiths were called Smith. Some people were named after where they lived. Some people lived by a river. They would be called River. Names became simple addresses. Nicknames were given. King was a name given to an important person. Children were given parents' names. Son of John became Johnson. They became older and got their own name.

Feedback ↻

Longer, more interesting sentences are created by joining two or more sentences with a connective. You should consider the different ways to vary sentences.

Objective ·····>

- To revise the language conventions and grammatical features of different kinds of texts.

Grammar Focus

- Written **reports** describe the way things are. They try to make the information as clear as possible to the reader.
- A report:
  - could be a guide book
  - could be a report on your project on dinosaurs
  - could be a description of a scene.
- Check that if you are writing a report, it has the following grammatical and language features:
  - an **introduction**
  - a **description** (which makes up most of the report)
  - a **conclusion**
  - uses mainly **action verbs**: *changes, falls*
  - uses the **present tense**
  - contains some **technical vocabulary**
  - is written in a **formal style** – perhaps in the third person.

Starter >

❶ Here is a report about bats:

In Britain there are fourteen species of bat. These bats live in the south and west of England. There are very few bats in Scotland. All the bats are small. On average they weigh 4 grams and have a wing span of 20cm. There are a few myths about bats. 'As blind as a bat' is completely wrong. Bats can see, but not in colour. Bats are under threat now more than most other wildlife.

ⓐ Copy the report. Underline the verbs. Which tense are they in?

ⓑ Write three pieces of detail given about bats that you could check in another reference book.

ⓒ Does the writer talk about one animal in particular or about bats generally? Which pronoun tells you this?

ⓓ Do you have to put your facts in a certain order when you are writing a report? Explain your answer.

ⓔ What kinds of diagrams would help you understand the information more clearly in this report?

Practice >>

2 This report sounds strange because the verbs are in the wrong tense. Rewrite it, putting the verbs into the present tense.

> Metals were an essential part of our lives. Most of the metals we used began their lives in the earth. An ore was a mixture of metal and other rock. When we made alloys we made it like toffee. We placed all the ingredients in a pan and heated it. The ore turned to liquid and was poured off. The process of extracting the metal from ore was called smelting.

3 Copy these sentences. Add suitable clauses to complete them.

(a) The match will not light again because ...
(b) Gas will cause an explosion if ...
(c) Water expands when freezing so ...
(d) It is best to plant seeds when ...
(e) Heavy objects will sink in water although ...

Extension >>>

4 Write your own report. Use one of these subjects.

(a) an entry from a book for parents about your school
(b) a report on your latest project
(c) a description of the scene outside the classroom window.

Try to follow this plan:
• Write a general opening about your subject.
• Include some more detail.
• Describe some things in real detail: functions, qualities, habits.
• Include a comparison with something else.
• Write a conclusion.

Feedback ↺

There are many kinds of report. To write in an appropriate style you need to be clear about its purpose and audience.

Check for the following grammatical and language features: an introduction, a description, a conclusion, verbs and tenses.

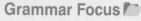

Objective ·····>

- To revise the language conventions and grammatical features of different kinds of texts.

Grammar Focus

- The purpose of a **recount** is to re-tell information or to give an **account of events**. It can be fiction or non-fiction. For example:

  – It could be a recount of a visit to a farm.

  – It could be a newspaper account.

  – It could be a biography.

- Amongst other things, check that your recounts contain the following:

  – a **clear order of events**

  – paragraphs to mark **changes in time**

  – a **conclusion**

  – '**Time**' **connectives**, such as 'meanwhile', 'later'.

Starter >

1 A feature of a recount is the use of the past tense. Copy the sentences. Change the verbs into the past tense.

(a) Tracy goes to nursery school every day. She learns how to write.

(b) I begin school in the autumn and leave the following term.

(c) Mike swims the river every year and climbs exhausted onto the bank.

(d) My mum forgets the sweets and gives me an apple.

(e) Jim writes the cheque and gives it to him.

(f) I forget my lunch so I eat a chocolate bar.

2 Another feature of a recount is writing events in chronological order (in the correct time sequence). Rewrite how to make toast, putting the events into the correct order.

(a) Finally, eat it!

(b) First, cut some bread.

(c) Then select the cooking time on the dial of the toaster.

(d) You need an electric toaster.

(e) When the toast pops up, remove it and butter it.

(f) Insert the bread.

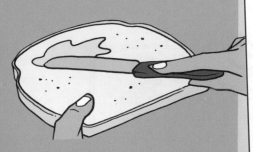

Practice >>

3 Copy the passage.

> The bank in the High Street was full of bored people. Robert and I stood in a queue and watched impatiently, when suddenly we saw a man in black barge through the doors.
>
> 'What shall we do?' I whispered.
>
> Before Robert could reply the alarm rang. Next the thief looked around him, threw down the bag and ran.
>
> This was a frightening experience that I would not like to live through again.

(a) Circle the pronouns. What do you notice?
(b) Underline the verbs. Which tense is used?
(c) What information does the writer give you? In what order is it given to you?
(d) How does the writer set the scene in the bank?
(e) Which people are involved? Are they named or left anonymous?
(f) Underline connectives and words which start the sentences.
(g) How do they help to move the recount forward?

Extension >>>

4 Choose one of these examples.

(a) A visit to ...
(b) A famous person we have studied in history is ...

Write your own recount text using these features:

* Set the scene.
* Describe events in order.
* Use 'I' or 'we' pronouns.
* Be accurate in your description of people.
* Use connectives such as: *'next'*, *'then'*, *'after that'*, *'finally'*
* Finish with a sentence which sums up the events.

Feedback ↻

Check for these features:

* an accurate title
* usually starts with setting the scene
* uses the past tense
* uses a variety of sentence beginnings
* includes many active verbs.

Unit 24: Explanation

Objective ·····⟩

- To revise the language conventions and grammatical features of different kinds of texts.

Grammar Focus

- **Explanations** are written to explain **how something works** or the **processes involved** in actions, events or behaviours. They can **explain** how to do something.

- They usually (but not always) start with a **general statement** to introduce the topic being explained

- They need to follow a set of **logical steps** – in a correct order – or else the process may not be clear or not work.

- They are usually written in the **present tense**.

- They are written in **chronological order**, i.e. the stages follow each other in the correct sequence in time.

- Explanations are used in subjects such as history and science.

Starter ⟩

1 Read the explanation below and answer the questions.

> Locks are built to control the flow of rivers. They let boats move up or down stream without losing water from the lock system, thus preventing water from being wasted. Locks are small and are usually made of two gates which are closed to let water escape or to pump it in. This is how boats can travel upstream. A series of locks is like a flight of stairs.

  ⓐ Copy the passage. Underline the verbs.
     What tense are they written in?

  ⓑ Explanations start with an introduction or introductory statement. What is the introductory statement in this passage?

  ⓒ Is there any order in the information written down?

  ⓓ What kinds of diagrams would improve the explanation?

  ⓔ Make up some questions about the passage beginning with 'what', 'how', 'why'.
     Why are the locks made of two gates?

  ⓕ Most explanations are written in an impersonal style. Is there anything 'personal' in this explanation? Would this be an appropriate style for this kind of writing?

Practice >>

2 Often, explanations use passive verbs. Copy this passage.
Change the verbs where possible into the passive form.

> The dog pulled Tom up the road. On his way to school Tom lingered in the park. When he arrived at school his teacher told him off for being late.

3 Copy these sentences. Add an appropriate beginning or end to each sentence. Join it to the rest of the sentence by using connectives to do with time: *then, next, after*

(a) Some people believe a meteor crashed to the earth …

(b) … the Ice Age arrived to kill the dinosaurs.

(c) … new animals evolved from the dinosaurs who had survived.

4 Copy these sentences and add an appropriate beginning or ending. Join it to the rest of the sentence by using a connective word or phrase to do with cause and effect: *because, so, this results in, therefore*

(a) Plants grow upwards …

(b) … is important to growth.

(c) If you do not give a plant enough sunlight …

(d) … we can prove the need for light.

Extension >>>

5 Write an explanation of your own, e.g. how to get your class computer to print out your work.

Use the following steps:

- Write an **introduction** to the topic.
- Explain each step in the process:
  - Step 1
  - Step 2
  - Step 3
- **Finish** the process.

Feedback ↩

If you are writing an explanation, check for the following features:

- a statement of what is to be explained at the beginning
- a description of the various parts or components involved
- a description of how and why something does something
- a summary at the end
- use of the present tense and action verbs: *rises, falls, changes*
- use of words to suggest cause and effect: *so, consequently, since.*

Unit 25: Instructions

Objective ·····>

- To revise the language conventions and grammatical features of different kinds of texts.

Grammar Focus

- When you give someone **instructions**, you describe how something is **made** or **done** in a **clear and ordered way**.

- Instructions are always linked with an activity. They exist to help people to carry out an action.

  – You could instruct someone how to get from your house to school.

  – You could write a recipe.

  – You could tell someone how to programme your video machine to record.

Starter >

❶ Rewrite these sentences. Change the verbs, where appropriate, into the imperative (command) form that is used in instructions.
'May I take a sweet?' becomes *'Take a sweet.'*
This may involve changing the sentences quite considerably.

ⓐ It is possible to switch off the computer.
ⓑ Fred can pull the joystick of his computer game.
ⓒ Would you like to have another biscuit?
ⓓ My teacher asked me to write out the spellings.
ⓔ The bus conductor asked me to sit down and be quiet.

❷ Rewrite these instructions. Use some of the connectives in the box to make them sound better.

Leave the house. Turn right. Walk for ten minutes. Turn left. Stop at the bus stop. Cross the road. Walk up the side street. Enter the market.

first	next	before	that	and
then	therefore	after	soon	

Practice >>

❸ Read the instructions.

Painting a wall

You need: a large paint brush, emulsion paint, protective clothing, coverings to protect furniture and carpet.

Procedure: Cover the floor and furniture before you begin. Limit yourself to a small area of wall so that the paint does not dry too quickly. Paint large areas a bit at a time. Paint vertical stripes first, then make cross strokes to join them. Do not put any more paint on your brush. Continue to smooth gently – back into the painted piece.

ⓐ Copy the instructions. Underline the verbs. Do instructions use a special form of the verb?

ⓑ How is this kind of writing set out differently from many other kinds of writing?

ⓒ Why is a list of equipment so important with instructions? Where should it be written in the instructions?

ⓓ Why is writing an event in the correct order so important in a set of instructions?

Extension >>>

❹ Write your own set of instructions. Choose one of these subjects:

ⓐ Instruct someone how to get from your house to school.
ⓑ Write instructions on how to make a paper aeroplane.
ⓒ Tell someone how to programme your video machine to record.

Follow these four steps:

- Write down what you are trying to do. Give your writing a title.
- Write a list of what you need. the materials or equipment needed.
- Write down the steps you need to take. Put these in the correct order.
- Decide whether a diagram would be helpful.

Feedback ↩

When writing instructions, check for the following features: a statement of the aim; a list of materials or anything else you require; a series of logical steps to describe a process; use of diagrams if necessary; use of the present tense; detailed information dealing with 'when', 'where' and 'how'; the use of the second person – 'you'; verbs to describe actions in the command form; link words to do with a time sequence; detailed factual description.

Objective ·····>

- To revise the language conventions and grammatical features of different kinds of texts.

Grammar Focus

- Often, in written discussions or arguments, you need to **persuade** your reader and make sure your **point of view** is clearly stated. Examples of persuasive writing include:

    – a letter to a newspaper disagreeing with foxhunting

    – an advertisement for a new pair of training shoes

    – a brochure trying to get someone to give you money for sick animals.

Starter >

❶ Read this letter about foxhunting.

> Foxhunting is cruel and I believe it should be banned. Every thinking person in this country knows they are hunted just for fun. To prove this, I talked to a shepherd last week who saw one defencelessly killed. Did you know the fox was really helping the country and is not a nuisance at all? In fact, it helps to keep down harmful pests.

(a) Copy the passage. Underline the opening statement.

(b) Is this a personal or an impersonal statement? Which words tell you?

(c) How many different arguments does the writer use?

(d) Underline the verbs. What tenses are used?

(e) List the kinds of connective words and phrases the writer uses. For example: **To prove this** ...

(f) What could you say in defence of foxhunting if someone objected to this argument?

Practice ≫

2 Copy the passage. Change the verbs in this argument to the simple present tense so that it sounds better. For example: *Cats **are** a nuisance.*

> Cats were a nuisance. They have continually dug up my flowerbeds and scratched my lawn. They needed to be kept in by their owners. If I saw another one in my garden I chased it away.

3 Write four more sentences to the argument, keeping to the appropriate tense.

4 Arguments (persuasive writing) often use logical connectives to prove their points:

therefore, showing that, however, because

Write some sentences of your own to do with an argument:
School uniform should/should not be worn.

Use some of the connectives in your argument.

Extension ≫≫

5 Write your own persuasive text and convince your reader that:
Smoking is bad for your health.

Follow this plan:
- Write an opening statement explaining your point of view.
- Make a point. Give some detail and a reason.
- Make another point. Give some detail and a reason.
- Make a further point. Give some detail and a reason.
- Use connectives such as:
  Indeed … However … For example … To conclude …
- Come back to your argument. Summarise your reasons.
- At the end show how you have proved your point by restating it:
  Therefore …

Feedback ↺

If you are writing texts to persuade, check for the following features:
- use of the third person if it is a formal argument
- use of the second person in advertising (it is more direct)
- active verbs in the present tense
- connectives intended to show logic:
  because, which shows that, therefore
- in advertising you tend to invent your own rules for punctuation in order to attract attention.

Objective ·····>

- To revise the language conventions and grammatical features of different kinds of texts.

Grammar Focus

- A **discussion** should present **all sides of an argument** to your reader, not just what you think.

- You will give arguments and information from **various points of view**. For example:

  I believe that school holidays are too long. However, I can understand that many people think children and teachers need a rest from each other.

- Discussions often use **reported speech**.

- Discussion uses **connectives** intended to show logic, for example:

  because, this shows, therefore

- Discussion states its case, provides a series of arguments and counter-arguments to be fair and then concludes with what the speaker believes.

Starter >

❶ Read this passage from a discussion.

> In Britain, road accidents to do with drink-driving are the commonest cause of death in young people. I believe that people who drink and drive are not only being stupid with their own lives but are also selfish because they endanger the lives of others. People can be crippled for life through no fault of their own.

ⓐ Copy the passage and underline the verbs.
   Which tense are they in?
ⓑ Underline the first sentence.
   How does it introduce the discussion?
ⓒ Write out one argument from the passage and the evidence that is given to prove it.

❷ Copy and complete these three sentences with a suitable ending. Note how the underlined connectives can make your argument stronger.

ⓐ Young drivers cause most accidents <u>because</u> ...
ⓑ They often drive faster <u>therefore</u> ...
ⓒ Many people think they should not drive alone <u>however</u> ...

Practice >>

3 Change this direct speech to reported speech. For example:

'Why do you want to smoke?' the teacher asked.
The teacher asked why he wanted to smoke.

(a) 'It doesn't make you look any more important,' my mum said.
(b) 'All Ranjit wants is to look cool,' said Reena.
(c) 'I smoke all the time with my friends,' boasted Jimmy.
(d) 'I think that you are wasting your time and money,' replied Chris.

Extension >>>

4 Write your own discussion of this topic:
'The arguments for and against children being given homework.'
Use the following plan to help:

- Explain the topic for discussion.
- Give one argument and some evidence.
- Give an opposing argument and some evidence.
- Give a second argument and some evidence.
- Give an opposing argument and some evidence.
- Say what you believe.
- Write your conclusion from all the evidence.

Feedback

If you are writing a discussion, check that it follows these conventions:

- tends to be personal in viewpoint so uses the first person
- often uses the present tense
- mostly uses active verbs, but can use passive verbs too.

Unit 28: Using standard English

Objective ·····>

- To use standard English consistently in formal situations and in writing.

Grammar Focus

- For centuries there have been many versions of spoken English.

  When the language started to be written down, rules were invented and **standard English** was said to be the correct version of written English.

  It is important to learn and use the rules of written language so that we can communicate more easily with each other.

  We have not got no money is not standard English.

  We haven't any money is standard English.

Starter >

1 Rewrite these sentences, using the correct form of the verbs.

(a) My two cats was/were asleep in the basket.
(b) Yesterday, my dad has/had a hard day at the office.
(c) We seen/saw him when he came/come to the club.
(d) Sophie done/did her homework last night.
(e) She should have/of taken/took more care with it.
(f) All the dogs was/were hungry but we wasn't/weren't.

Practice »

2 Copy and complete the sentences.
Choose the correct word from the box to fill the gap.

there	*its*	*anything*	*quiet*	*two*
their	*it's*	*neither*	*herself*	*too*
they're	*nothing*	*quite*	*themselves*	*to*

(a) Over ____ are my ____ cats asleep in ____ chair.
(b) ____ a shame I do not have my camera.
(c) She didn't know ____ about it.
(d) Shh! You have to be ____ in a library.
(e) They helped ____ to my lunch.
(f) Tracy is ____ shy ____ be a TV presenter.
(g) My dog has been known to chase ____ tail for ___ a time.

3 Use the words in the box you have not used in some sentences of your own.

Extension »»

4 Write out this passage in standard English.

Me boat was ran aground off of the coast. It had been damaged by a ship what reversed into it and sailed off more faster than us. It were a good job that my dad had learned me how to row a boat. We was stuck in the sea for a day without no food. Them people who say you can do without no drink for this long time should of been with us. They could of took charge. There is not many things you can do if you've not got no food left.

REMEMBER

The use of English depends upon the context and to whom you are speaking.

Feedback ↻

Non-standard English is often used in everyday speech. In formal situations, it is best to use standard English. In writing we usually need to use standard English.

Objective ·····>

- To investigate the differences between spoken and written language.

Grammar Focus

- For centuries there have been many versions of spoken English. When the language was written down, rules were invented and **standard English** was said to be the correct version of written English.

- Some words and expressions are only used by people in a certain area or country, e.g. cockney **dialect** words from London and words from the USA. These are dialect words and are not standard English. We often use these words in speech, but not normally in formal writing.

Starter >

❶ Match the cockney rhyming dialect words to their standard English version. Write them out.

Cockney dialect	Standard English
(a) trouble and strife	legs
(b) bacon and eggs	hat
(c) plates of meat	tea
(d) this and that	wife
(e) pot and pan	talk
(f) rabbit and pork	feet
(g) Rosie Lee	man

❷ Would you use these words in spoken or written English? Say why.

Practice >>

3 Copy and complete the chart.
Use a dictionary and other reference sources to help.

American dialect word	Standard English
elevator	lift
apartment	
trunk of a car	
caretaker	
game of draughts	
ice-box	
subway	
movie	
gas	
thumbtacks	

4 Which of these words are becoming more commonly used in English?

Extension >>>

5 Rewrite this Cockney poem in standard English.
Say it to yourself first and listen how the words sound.

Wot a marf 'e'd got, ⟶ What a mouth he had got
Wot a marf.
When 'e wos a kid
Goo' Lor' luv'er
'Is pore old muvver
Must 'a' fed 'im wiv a shuvvle,
Wot a gap 'e'd got
Pore chap,
'E'd never been known to larf,
'Cos if 'e did
It's a penny to a quid ⟶ I bet you a penny to a pound
'E'd 'a' split 'is face in arf.

6 Say which of the two versions
you prefer and why.

Feedback ↩

There is a difference between speaking and writing.
When people speak they use body language and
facial expressions. Writing is more impersonal and
clues to meaning have to be supplied by the writer.

Objective ·····>

- To identify ways in which sentence structure, language and punctuation are different in older texts.

Grammar Focus

- This unit looks at the history of the English language. Because Britain has been invaded so many times over the centuries and has traded with so many countries, new words have been introduced. This makes our language very rich and interesting. For example:

  – From the Romans we got Latin words such as 'century' and 'audio'.

  – From the Greeks we got new science words such as 'microscope' and 'biology'.

  – The French left us with new word endings such as 'age' in 'garage' and 'et' in 'ballet'.

  – The Vikings left us with short, hard-sounding words such as 'skirt' and 'knife'.

Starter >

❶ Copy and complete the chart to show the influence of Latin and Greek words in English.

Latin or Greek	Meaning	Two examples of words
nova (Latin)	new	novel, novelty
photo (Greek)	light	
bi (Latin)		bicycle
-ology (Greek)	a study of	
centum (Latin)		century
bio (Greek)	life	
micro (Greek)		microscope
audio (Latin)		audible

Practice >>

2 Read and copy this passage written by William Caxton in 1490.

And the good wyfe answerde that she coude speke no frenshe. And the marchaunt was angry for he also coude speke no frenshe, but wold have hadde egges and she understode hym not. And thenne at laste a nother sayd that he wolde have eyren*. Then the good wyf sayd that she understod hym wel.

* a local word for eggs.

(a) Underline the words which you cannot understand.
(b) Where could you look to find out about them?
(c) Underline the words you can understand but which are spelled differently today.
(d) Which words show that there were no spelling rules in those days?
(e) Write a modern version of the passage explaining what the problem was.

Extension >>>

3 Copy the passage from Shakespeare's play *Macbeth*. It was written four hundred years ago.

First witch: Round about the cauldron go;
  In the poisoned entrails throw,
  Toad that under cold stone
  Days and nights hath thirty one
  Swelter'd venom sleeping got,
  Boil thou first i' th' charmed pot.

All: Double, double, toil and trouble;
  Fire burn and cauldron bubble.

(a) Say how you know this passage is from a play.
(b) What are the witches doing when they are saying these words?
(c) Why do you think Shakespeare chose to rhyme this speech?
(d) Underline any words you do not understand.
(e) See if you can find the words in a modern dictionary.
(f) What makes this more difficult to understand: the words used or the way the lines are written?
(g) Write a modern version of this scene.

Feedback ↩

Over the years we have taken words and grammar from many different countries. Reading Shakespeare shows us just how language changes over time. Lots of new words continually enter our language and others drop out of use or change their meaning.

Published by Letts Educational
The Chiswick Centre
414 Chiswick High Road
London W4 5TF
Tel: 020 89963333
Fax: 020 87428390
email: mail@lettsed.co.uk
website: www.letts-education.com

Letts Educational Limited is a division of Granada Learning Limited, part of the Granada Media Group.
© Ray Barker and Louis Fidge 2002
First published 2002

ISBN 1 84085 667 X

British Library Cataloguing in Publication Data
A catalogue record for this book is available from the British Library.

Acknowledgements

The publishers would like to thank the following for permission to use copyright material. Every effort has been made to trace copyright holders and to obtain their permission for the use of copyright material. The author and publishers will gladly receive information enabling them to rectify any error or omission in subsequent editions.
Illustrations: Topham Picturepoint pages 54, 55 and 62

Commissioned by Helen Clark
Project management by Vicky Butt and Aetos Ltd
Editing by Diana Roberts and Jane Otto
Cover design by Bigtop Design
Internal design by Aetos Ltd
Illustrations by Sylvie Poggio Artists Agency: Nick Duffy, Tony Forbes and Roger Langridge
Production by PDQ
Printed in the UK by Ashford Colour Press